REUDOR's THE DOODLE FAMILY™

the Hebrew Months tell their Story

Text & Verse: **Reudor**   Art: **Reudor, Jack Knight**

PITSPOPANY

NEW YORK ◆ JERUSALEM

Meet The Doodles

Bitsy

Oody

Poodly

Trudy

Also in this Series: THE HEBREW LETTERS TELL THEIR STORY

Published by Pitspopany Press
Text and art copyright © 2000 by Reudor. All rights reserved.
All characters featured in this publication are trademarks of Atara Publishing.
No part of this book may be translated, reproduced or transmitted in any form or by any means,
electronic or mechanical, including photocopying, recording, or by any information storage and
retrieval system, without permission in writing from the publisher.

PITSPOPANY PRESS books may be purchased for educational or special sales by contacting:
Marketing Director, Pitspopany Press, 40 East 78th Street, Suite 16D, New York, New York 10021.
Tel: (800) 232-2931 Fax: (212) 472-6253
Email: pop@netvision.net.il
Web Site: www.pitspopany.com

Hardcover ISBN: 1-930143-04-4
Softcover ISBN: 1-930143-05-2

Printed in Hong Kong

Where to Find What

Do you know when Hanukkah is? Or Passover? Do you know the date of your Hebrew birthday? Simple, it's all there in the Hebrew calendar: the new moon, candle lighting times - everything! But what did people do before there was a printed calendar?

A CALENDAR

The New Month

In ancient times the people of Israel watched the skies for the appearance of the new moon, signifying the beginning of a new month. As soon as it was spotted, great bonfires were lit on the hill tops to spread the news, beginning with Jerusalem's Mount of Olives and on as far as the Babylonian frontier. The Sanhedrin (the highest court of law) fixed the dates of the holidays and the festivals, giving some months twenty nine days and others thirty days. Fast messengers relayed the information.

But Jews in far-off countries, like Persia and Italy and Egypt, could not rely on messages which sometimes arrived very late. In order to be sure, they observed both the thirtieth day AND the day after it as the new month - just in case!

Since then, tradition dictates that in places outside of Israel, an extra day is added to Passover, Shavuot, and Sukkot holidays.

Moon-Month and Sun-Year

Now a new problem arose. Twelve moon months added up to 354 days. That meant that at times, Passover would be celebrated in the winter instead of the spring, and planting seasons would have been totally confused!

The people watched the sun closely, and discovered that a year calculated by the sun has 365 days.

4

"We must devise a plan to keep the moon-month in step with the sun-year," the astronomers said. So they arranged a leap year which had an additional month after Adar, called Adar Sheni (Second Adar), which comes every two to three years.

And so, the Hebrew calendar is both a lunar (moon) and solar (sun) calendar.

The Written Calendar

Over time, our people were driven out of the Jewish homeland. Jews were scattered to the four corners of the earth. There was no central Jewish community and no chief authority with regard to religious laws and customs. So it became necessary to have a written calendar.

In the year 359 C.E., Rabbi Hillel the Second set down the rules for making a calendar. The year count starts from the day the world was created. The Jewish day begins at sunset, because the Bible tells us, in the story of the Creation, that "there was evening and there was morning, one day." The very first day began not with daybreak but with sunset. All our holidays follow this order and begin at sunset of the day before.

From that day forth, all Jews everywhere could determine the calendar for themselves and observe the festivals on the same day.

Our calendar today has remained the same since that time!

Elul אלול
August
Av אב
July
Tammuz תמוז
June
Sivan סיון
May
Iyar אייר
April
Nissan ניסן

TISHRAY

Every month has its season,
Every time has a reason:
A time to laugh, a time to cry,
A time for hello, a time for good-bye.
There's time to work, there's time to play,
Time for night and time for day.
There's time to slide and time to climb,
Time for a quarter, time for a dime.

LIBRA

IN THE MONTH OF TISHRAY

- There are more holidays and festivals than in any other month: Rosh Hashanah, Yom Kippur, Sukkot, Hoshanah Rabah, Shmini Atzeret, and Simhat Torah!

- It is the first month in the modern Hebrew calendar, and the seventh month according to the Torah.

שרי

You can take your time or give it away,
Time to shower in April or flower in May.
There is time to catch and time to pitch,
Time to scratch and time to itch.
There's time to think
and time to decide,
There's time through the middle
and time on the side.
There's time for lemon,
there's time for lime,
And now it's time
to do the next rhyme...

7

• The name comes from a Babylonian word for "beginning".

• It is also known as Yerah Ha'Aytanim, Month of the Mighty, since
Abraham, Isaac, and Jacob were all born during Tishray.

• The sign of Libra signifies this period when we're being judged,
our good deeds tipping the scales in our favor.

AUTUMN

Rosh Hashanah

Two important things take place on Rosh Hashanah:

1. We celebrate God's greatness and absolute power.
2. We are being judged for all of our actions.

As a way for us to remember God and repent for our sins, the shofar, ram's horn, is sounded one hundred times (one hundred and one times in Sephardic communities)! The blowing of the shofar reminds both the Jewish people and God, of Abraham's willingness to sacrifice his son, Isaac, to fulfill God's command. The Torah reading for the second day of the holiday tells that story.

During Rosh Hashanah we wish each other:
"May you be inscribed in the Book of Life",
and people send greeting cards to family and friends.

On the first day the ceremony of tashlich takes place. The community gathers by a pond or a river, and symbolically casts off sins by tossing bread crumbs into the water.

The festive meal includes dipping challa and apples in honey, in the hope of a sweet year. It is customary to eat a pomegranate and say, "May our merits be as plentiful as the seeds of a pomegranate."

In some communities, the head of a fish is placed on the table as we celebrate Rosh Hashanah, the Head of the Year.

Have a Sweet Year!

YOM KIPPUR

Before the arrival of Yom Kippur,
the custom of kaparot, symbolic
attonments, may be performed.
Using a live chicken or money,
the parent waves it over
the head of each child,
asking God for mercy, and then giving the money to charity.

Yom Kippur is the day when the judgments for the coming year are sealed, and there are three things that can help us avoid any decrees against us:

repentance,
            prayer,
                    and charity.

On Yom Kippur Eve the concluding meal is eaten, and a fast begins which lasts twenty five hours. Many people wear white, because on this day Jews are likened to angels. The story of Jonah and the Great Fish is told.

SUKKOT

Sukkot was the most important festival during biblical times. It was simply referred to as THE festival, and was chosen by King Solomon for the dedication of the Temple. It was also called Hag HaAsif, the festival of ingathering, when the harvest was celebrated, and Z'man Simhataynu, the season for our happiness.

We build a temporary hut - a Sukkah, which resembles the huts the Israelites lived in during their wanderings through the desert. We cover the Sukkah with tree branches, and decorate the walls with fruit, pictures and crafts. During the holiday we eat in the Sukkah, and some people actually sleep in it!

A special ceremony is performed over a bouquet of the four kinds of growing things:

lulav (palm branch),
hadasim (myrtle),
aravot (willows),
and etrog (citrus).

The custom of inviting guests to visit the Sukkah adds to the fun, as well as symbolic guests, such as Abraham, Isaac, Jacob, Joseph, Moses, Aaron and David - one for each day.

The seventh day of Sukkot is called Hoshanah Rabah. On this day the judgment made on Rosh Hashanah and Yom Kippur is finalized, and there is a custom is to beat willow branches on the floor.

10

Simhat Torah

Shmini Atzeret is the day following Sukkot. During that day the prayers for rain begin, and we can ask God for our personal needs.

Immediately after is the happy occasion of Simhat Torah, celebrating the completion of the five books of the Torah.

There is much singing and dancing in honor of the Torah, while circling around the synagogue. Children wave flags, reminiscent of the tribal flags under which the Israelites marched in the desert. Sometimes a cored apple is placed on top of the flag pole, with a lighted candle in the hole, as the Torah is likened to light.

During the morning synagogue service, the children are called up to the Torah; the only time that such a custom occurs.

The first Sabbath after Simhat Torah is called Shabbat Beraysheet, because on that Sabbath we begin reading the Torah all over again, starting from Beraysheet, the book of Genesis.

HESHVAN

12

SCORPIO

IN THE MONTH OF HESHVAN:

- On the seventh day, the prayers for rain begin.
- The Ark set sail. It rained for 40 days, nearly destroying the world. For a while, Heshvan was known as the month of Bul, short for Mabul (flood, in Hebrew).

חשון

Two by two, two by two,
Cats and gnats and ding bats too,
Ferrets, parrots, cockatoo
All the way from Timbuktu!
To the Ark they march together
To escape the nasty weather,
Wearing wool or fur or feather
Look - a monkey in a sweater!

In this month there came a flood,
Lots of rain and lots of mud,
Every roof and wall and stud
Came down crashing with a thud!
God said, "Noah's Ark I'll save,
Floating high on top the wave".
The rainbow then to us he gave
To remind us to behave!

13

• Rachel, one of the mothers of the Jewish people, died giving birth to Benjamin. She was buried on the way to Efrat, near Bethlehem, where her tomb stands to this day.

• Just like the world thirsts for rain during this month, so a scorpion, who lives in the desert, is always seeking water.

AUTUMN

KISLEV

A zillion leaves
Across the yard
I can't believe
We worked so hard.
We pile them high
We rake and rake,
Piled to the sky,
We need a break!

We need to rest
From such a pile,
Perhaps it's best
We play a while!
A zillion leaves
Across the yard,
I think that we've
Played way too hard...

14

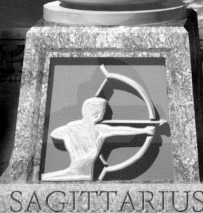

SAGITTARIUS

IN THE MONTH OF KISLEV

- The days grow short and nights arrive early, as the last month of Autumn prepares us for Winter.

- The first five days of Hanukkah are celebrated.

מסלי

AUTUMN

15

- The zodiac sign, Sagittarius, Keshet in Hebrew, means both rainbow and bow. It was in the beginning of Kislev when the rainbow appeared to Noah (see page12). And it was in Kislev that the Maccabees used their bows and belief in God to drive away the enemies of Israel.

HANUKKAH

When Alexander the Great conquered Judea, he let the Jewish inhabitants live according to their traditions. After his death, the country was taken over by the Syrian Greeks, under the leadership of Antiochus. The evil king insisted that the Jews must give up their religious life - and many did. Those Jews, who were called Hellenists, accepted the Greek culture and assimilated. They changed their traditions, dress, and even their language.

The Hasmonean family came from the town of Modiin to lead the Jewish people. They were headed by the Kohen Mattityahu and his five sons. Under the military leadership of the son Judah, they fought against Greek influence and rule. The Hasmoneans eventually beat the enemy, and the nation was once again free. They were also called Maccabees: as Mattityahu gathered his followers, he proclaimed, "Who is like you among the gods, Lord!" The Hebrew acronym is Maccabee. Another reason for the name may be the actual Hebrew meaning of the word, hammer, referring to Judah's strength with which he slammed the enemy.

Today we celebrate Hanukkah not only for the miracle of the victory against such a powerful enemy, but for another miracle. When the Temple was repaired and rededicated, only a small jug of oil was found to light the menorah, hardly enough to last a day. But the oil lasted for EIGHT days!

Before the holiday was referred to as Hanukkah (dedication), it was called the Festival of Lights, and sometimes the Festival of Fire.

Over the years, many traditions developed in the celebration of the holiday:

- We light the hanukkiyah for eight nights, say special prayers and sing songs.

- We play with a spinning top called draydel.

- We eat latkes (potato pancakes) and sufganiyot (jelly donuts).

- We give (and get!) money and presents.

16

Here is how some of these traditions got started:

In Middle Eastern countries Jewish parents gave their children candles shaped like a hand, called hamsa (five, in Arabic), signifying good luck.

In Eastern Europe, the fifth night of Hanukkah is the special one. On that evening, the family prepares a feast and celebrates the triumph of light over darkness since five candles are lit and only three still remain in darkness.

In Syria, instead of a traditional holiday meal, they have a sweet table stacked high with pastries and treats. Many guests come and enjoy the festival.

Yemenite children go to Hanukkah parties and bring roasted corn, carrots and grape juice.

In Kurdistan, children carried dolls of Antiochus, and at nightfall they set the dolls on fire.

Every year on the first night of Hanukkah, in the town of Modiin, a torch is lit at the Maccabee family tomb. The torch is relayed in a running race to Jerusalem and then to other parts of Israel.

The game of Draydel was used during the rule of Antiochus Epiphanes before the Maccabee revolt. During this time, any Jew who studied Torah would be executed. When children gathered to study and soldiers came by, the children quickly took out draydels and played. (These days, it's the other way around: if you're playing Draydel when you should be doing homework, you have to quickly put your Draydel away when your parents come by!)

Merchants brought Draydels from India to Europe during the Middle Ages. Germans adopted the custom of playing the Draydel Game, and created the traditional markings, N, G, H, S, which stood for Nichts (nothing), Ganz (all), Halb (half), and Stell ein (put in). They also named the game, calling it Drehen meaning turn. The game became so popular, children throughout Europe used to cast their own draydels out of lead.

In Hebrew, the Draydel is called a S'vivon (spinner). The German markings were changed to Hebrew. Nun, Gimel, Hey, Shin stand for *Ness Gadol Ha-ya Sham*: "a great miracle happened there." In Israel, they changed *there* to *here*, since the miracle happened in Israel.

The custom of giving coins to the kids actually began in Poland, where parents gave children money to give to their teachers on Hanukkah. Eventually, parents also gave some of this gelt to their children as a small reward for performing the task and for studying.

In the eighth century, poor yeshiva students began going door to door to receive money so they could continue studying.

When the last Maccabee son, Simon, became the High Priest, he was allowed to make his own coins for the Jewish State - a true sign of independence. We carry on this triumph today by giving coins.

TEVET

Our trusty dog will pull the sled,
As we explore the frozen North,
Through ice and snow, full speed ahead,
On this cold month, Tevet, the fourth.
We got provisions on the go,
Got cookies, cocoa and some cake,
We've made one hundred balls of snow
In case we meet a polar snake.

IN THE MONTH OF TEVET

- The last three days of Hanukkah are celebrated.
- On the eight day, the first Greek translation of the Torah was completed.
- On the ninth day, 2,500 years ago, Ezra the Scribe, who led Israel during the return from Babylonia, died.

CAPRICORN

We must have walked a million miles,
The squishy snow beneath our boots.
We looked at danger with our smiles
And didn't mess our new snow suits.
We climbed the tallest icy peak,
We conquered all of Wintertime!
Stop! That sound! Did someone speak?
Oh...It's Mom...It's dinnertime.

- On the tenth day, in 588 B.C.E., the Babylonians lay siege to Jerusalem. Today a fast day commemorates that event.

- Maimonides (Rabbi Moses Ben Maimon), the great philosopher and scholar, died on the twentieth day in 1204.

- The zodiac sign is a reminder that good times will soon return, and we'll be dancing around with joy, like young goats.

WIN

SHVAT

God said, "I made
This Earth for you,
With trees to shade
And house you, too.
I made the soil
To give you food,
Don't let it spoil,
Treat it real good!"

This land is ours,
To use with care.
The trees, the flowers,
The stream, the air.
And as she blooms
Be sure to treat her
Just like your room -
But only neater...

20

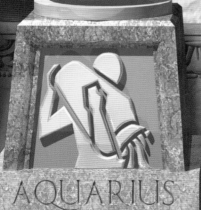

AQUARIUS

IN THE MONTH OF SHVAT

- On the first day Moses started to deliver his final address to Israel, as told in the book of Deuteronomy.

- The Ten Plagues against the Egyptians began.

- On the fifteenth day, Tu B'Shvat is celebrated.

שְׁבָט

21

- We pray for a beautiful Etrog to grow for Sukkot (see page 10).
- The Zodiac sign of Aquarius signifies the importance of water, especially on this month when we celebrate growing things.

WINTER

When God was creating the holidays, the Acacia tree said, "There should be a holiday in my honor, since my wood was used to make the ark which holds the Ten Commandments!"

Said the Cedar, "A holiday should be made for me, since King Solomon built the Temple with my wood!"

"You're both wrong," announced the Willow, "When the Israelites were exiled to Babylonia they sat by me for comfort. I deserve the honor!"

Said the Palm, "My branches are used during the Sukkot holiday."

"So is my fruit!" argued the Citron.

"King David played on a harp made from my branches!" reminded them the Cypress.

"Without me Noah would not have been able to build the ark," insisted the Gopher tree.

"My leaves dressed Adam and Eve," said the Fig tree.

"My fruit lit the Menorah!" proclaimed the Olive tree.

And so all the trees made their arguments.

Finally, God said, "You are all right. From the lowliest Bramble bush in which I appeared to Moses in fire, to the mighty Oak, all are dear to Me and worthy of a celebration."

And so He created Tu B'Shvat as Rosh Hashanah for ALL the trees.

The Sabbath of Tu B'Shvat is called Shabbat Shira - the Sabbath of Song. A nice custom is to leave food for birds on that day, in appreciation for their songs.

In ancient Israel a tree would be planted in a newborn child's honor: cedar for a boy, cypress for a girl. The child would care for the tree until married, when branches from it would be used for the *huppah* (canopy) during the wedding ceremony.

The Kabbalists in the northern city of Tzfat had a seder ceremony on Tu B'Shvat, similar to Passover. They sampled fifteen types of fruit and nuts, and drank four cups of wine, representing the four seasons: white for winter, rose for spring, red for summer, and blush for fall.

In Eastern European schools, kids brought figs, raisins, dates and carob, celebrating the fruit of trees common to ancient Israel.

In Kurdistan sweet fruits were placed around trees, and prayers were said for an abundant fruit season and many children.

During the 16th century in Sephardic communities, Ma-ot Perot (money for fruit) was raised to provide fruit for the poor.

In 1949, "Forest of the Martyrs" was established in Israel, where the goal is to plant six million trees in memory of the victims of the Holocaust. Tree planting ceremonies are plentiful in Israel on Tu B'Shvat, and are becoming more popular around the Jewish world. It has become a favorite day for nature strolls and picnics.

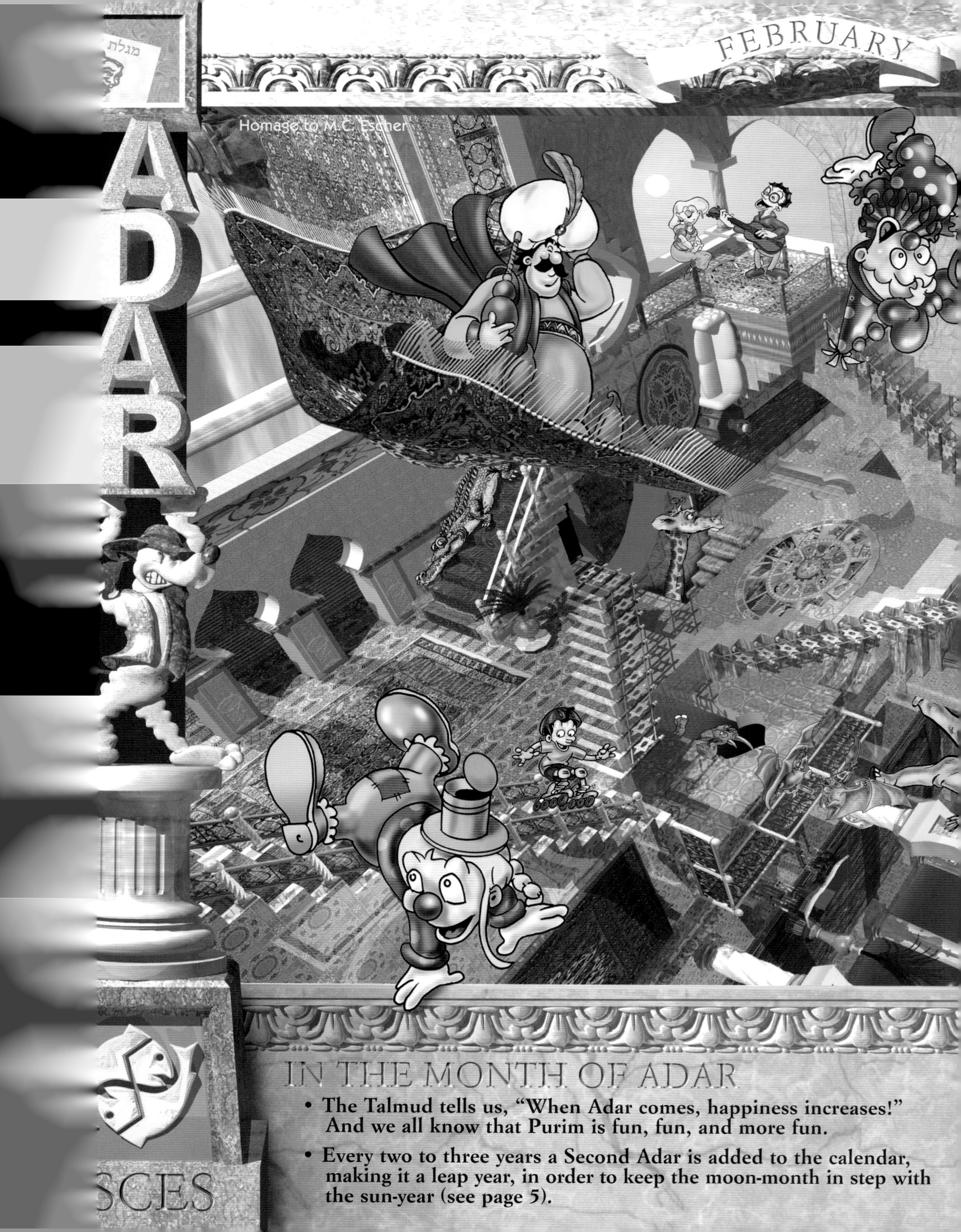

Homage to M.C. Escher

ADAR

PISCES

IN THE MONTH OF ADAR

- The Talmud tells us, "When Adar comes, happiness increases!" And we all know that Purim is fun, fun, and more fun.

- Every two to three years a Second Adar is added to the calendar, making it a leap year, in order to keep the moon-month in step with the sun-year (see page 5).

Adar
has come!
Adar is here!
It's time for
fun and feast.

Come all from far, come all from near,
Come all from West and East!
Laugh and sing and cross your eyes,
Twist and shake and shout,
Toot a flute and squeak like mice, dress up inside out!

Dance a jig up on the ceiling, floating off the floor,
This is such a thrilly feeling up above the door.
Dancing, prancing upside down In a clown suit,
On Adar we never frown. This month is a hoot!

25

- On the seventh day the greatest Jewish leader of all time, Moses, was born. On the same day, 120 years later, he died.

- On the tenth day, in 1475 in Italy, the first printed Hebrew book was published. It was Rashi's commentary on the Torah.

- Pisces, the fish, are nourished and supported by the sea, just like the "sea" of the Torah nourishes and supports the Jewish people.

WINTER

Purim

When Esther wins a beauty contest and becomes queen, her guardian, Mordechai, warns her not to reveal her Jewish heritage to King Ahashverosh. Mordechai, a proud leader of the Jews of Persia, brings on himself the wrath of Haman, the king's top advisor, by refusing to bow down to him. Haman convinces the king that the Jews are his enemies, and the king gives him permission to have them destroyed. Meanwhile, Mordechai foils a plan by two palace servants to assassinate the king, and the incident is recorded in the state chronicles. While Haman organizes his murderous scheme, he draws a lot (Purim means lots), to decide when to kill the Jews. He also erects a tall gallows to hang Mordechai on. But when Haman's plan becomes known, Esther intervenes. Since the queen was not allowed to speak to the king without special permission first, Esther knows that she's endangering her life. But the king listens to her plea, and hangs Haman on the gallows he prepared for Mordechai. He then appoints Mordechai as his top advisor, and the Jews are given permission to destroy all their enemies! Today we celebrate Purim as a happy reminder of those events!

IT IS CUSTOMARY TO GIVE PRESENTS TO THE POOR, AS WELL AS *MISHLOAH MANOT*, SENDING GIFTS OF FOOD TO FRIENDS. THE MOST POPULAR PASTRIES ARE HAMANTASCHEN, KNOWN IN HEBREW AS HAMAN'S EARS!

As a reward to Mordechai for saving his life, King Ahashverosh commands Haman to dress Mordechai in the finest clothes and lead him on horseback around the town, proclaiming Mordechai's greatness.

WHEN THE EVIL *HAMAN* IS MENTIONED DURING THE READING OF THE STORY OF *ESTHER*, WE USE NOISE MAKERS, CALLED GROGGERS, TO DROWN OUT HIS NAME.

NISSAN

ARIES

28

IN THE MONTH OF NISSAN

- On the first day, the Tabernacle was built in the desert. Years later, on the same day, the Second Temple was dedicated in Jerusalem.

- Isaac, one of the Forefathers of the Jewish people, was born. The sign of Aries reminds us of the ram which was sacrificed in Isaac's place.

Ring-a-ding!
Ding-a-ling!
I want to sing:
"Hooray for Spring!"
Kite on string,
Flight on swing,
I want to sing:
"Hooray for Spring!"

No snow nor freeze,
Just gentle breeze
Blows through the leaves
With perfect ease.
Let's climb up trees
(Don't scrape your knees),
And please oh please
DON'T TEASE THE BEES!

29

- On the tenth day, Miriam, sister of Moses and Aaron, died.

- In the Torah Nissan is called The First Month. It is also called the Month of Spring: Nitzan, Hebrew for flower bud, refers to the time when flowers bloom.

- On the twenty-seventh day is Yom Ha'Shoah, Holocaust Remembrance Day.

SPRING

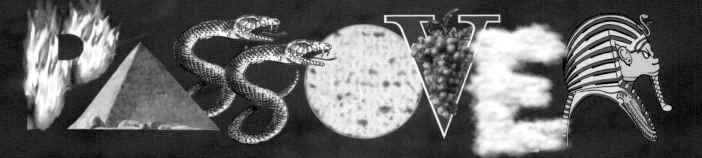

The Jewish people were slaves in Egypt for a long time. God sent Moses to tell Pharaoh:

"Let my people go!"

When Pharaoh refused, God punished the Egyptians with ten plagues. The plagues were meant for the Egyptians only. During the final plague the Angel of Death passed over the homes of the Israelites, which is the reason why the holiday is called Passover.

Pharaoh finally agreed to let them go. The Israelites hurried before he changed his mind, and there wasn't even time for the bread they baked to rise. Today we eat matzah on Passover to remind us of that bread.

The Israelites left in the middle of the night, and as they arrived at the Sea of Reeds, known as the Red Sea, they saw Pharaoh and his army chasing after them. At God's command, Moses placed his staff on the water, and the sea parted. No sooner did the freed slaves cross, then the Egyptians followed. But at that moment the sea crashed on top of them and the enemy of Israel drowned.

Now, as a nation, the freed slaves walked through the desert to receive God's law, and go into their own homeland.

Different communities around the world have their own cool ways of celebrating Passover:

Moroccan Jews wear long white robes on the Seder night to symbolize freedom. They also take a staff in their hands, place the wrapped Afikoman over their shoulders and walk a few paces with it, literally following the words in the Torah.

The rugged mountain Jews of Caucasus listen to their Elders read the Haggadah, while dressed in their best clothing and armed with weapons.

In Mexico, Jews would smear blood of a lamb on the doorposts, then gather by a stream and beat the water with willows, to remember Moses.

In Yemen, the women bake fresh matzah every day.

Libyan Jews recite Hallel while baking the matzot, just as it had been done every Passover during sacrifices, throughout Temple times.

In some Chasidic communities, the Lulav used during Sukkot (see page 10) is used to light the fire for burning Chametz.

The Men of the Great Assembly were the first to write the Haggadah Story down, in 300 B.C.E. Today there are more than 3,000 known published editions of the Passover Haggadah, including The Energizing Haggadah and The Doodle Family Haggadah!

IYAR

I saw it streak across the sky,
It was a shooting star!
I saw it flying really high,
This eighteenth of Iyar.
I heard that shooting stars like this
Will make a wish come true:
"I wish it turned my noisy sis
Into a kangaroo!"

32

TAURUS

IN THE MONTH OF IYAR

- On the first day, construction of both the first and second Temples began.

- The name Iyar comes from the Hebrew word *Or*, (light). In the Book of Kings it is called the month of Ziv, also meaning light.

- Yom Ha'Atzmaut and Lag B'Omer are celebrated (see next page).

SPRIN

"I wish to get a bouncing ball,
A room to call my own",
"I wish for peace to come to all"
"I wish for a juicy bone".
I think I saw a shooting star
Streak across the sky.
I think it was a shooting star...
Or just a firefly.

33

- On the twenty-eighth day, Yom Yerushalayim, Jerusalem Day, is celebrated, commemorating the liberation of Jerusalem during the Six Day War in 1967.

- The Israel Defense Forces are likened to Taurus the bull, charging into its enemies.

SPRING

ISRAEL INDEPENDENCE DAY

God's promise to Abraham was fulfilled when the Israelites, led by Joshua, conquered the land of Canaan after wandering throughout the desert.

King David secured Israel's borders and built Jerusalem as the nation's capital, leaving to his son, Solomon, a thriving and powerful country. But after Solomon's death, a revolt broke out and the country was split into two kingdoms, Israel and Judea.

Over time the kingdoms were destroyed by the Assyrians and Babylonians, and the people were carried off into captivity.

Under Persian rule, Jews were allowed back into their land. With the victory of the Hasmoneans over the Syrian Greeks (see page 16), Israel again became free and powerful. But 200 years later, in 63 B.C.E. the Romans invaded, and once again Israel lost its independence.

But 1,884 years later, on the fifth day in the month of Iyar, May 14, 1948, the State of Israel was proclaimed in Tel Aviv. Ten minutes later, the five surrounding Arab states, with help from other countries, attacked the Jewish state from the land, sea and air. Israel drove off its enemies, and each year Yom Ha'Atzmaut, Independence Day, is celebrated, first with memorial ceremonies and then with dancing in the streets, fireworks, parades, and parties.

LAG B'OMER

The counting of the Omer starts when the first of the new grain harvest was brought to the Temple on the second day of Passover (see page 29). The counting concludes forty-nine days later, during the late harvest of Shavuot (see page 38).

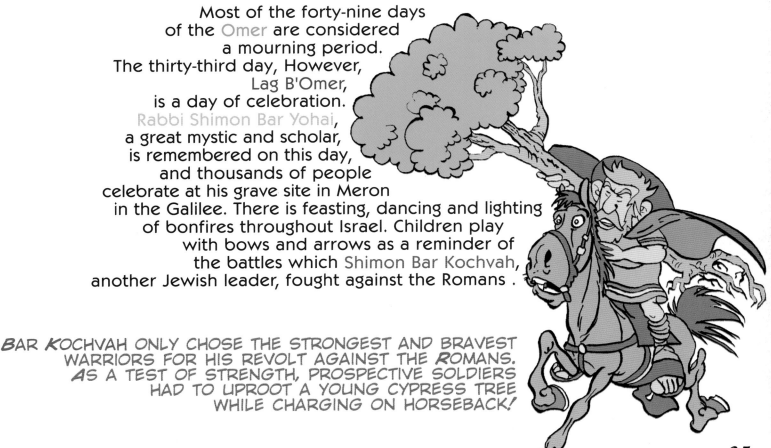

Most of the forty-nine days of the Omer are considered a mourning period. The thirty-third day, However, Lag B'Omer, is a day of celebration. Rabbi Shimon Bar Yohai, a great mystic and scholar, is remembered on this day, and thousands of people celebrate at his grave site in Meron in the Galilee. There is feasting, dancing and lighting of bonfires throughout Israel. Children play with bows and arrows as a reminder of the battles which Shimon Bar Kochvah, another Jewish leader, fought against the Romans .

BAR KOCHVAH ONLY CHOSE THE STRONGEST AND BRAVEST WARRIORS FOR HIS REVOLT AGAINST THE ROMANS. AS A TEST OF STRENGTH, PROSPECTIVE SOLDIERS HAD TO UPROOT A YOUNG CYPRESS TREE WHILE CHARGING ON HORSEBACK!

SIVAN

When The Temple stood so proud
In this summer month, Sivan,
Down the road a happy crowd
Travels in a caravan.
From their farms across the land,
carrying their harvest best,
There's a gift in every hand,
There is room for every guest.

And today here on the farm,
Celebrating this tradition,
Country air and country charm
And a lesson in nutrition:
Dairy, vegetables, and fruit
We shall eat during Sivan,
Do you hear a hooting-toot?
Let's go catch the ice cream van!

36

GEMINI

IN THE MONTH OF SIVAN

- On the sixth day, the Torah was given to Israel.
- On the sixth day, King David was born - and seventy years later, died.
- On the sixth day, Baby Moses was found floating in a basket on the Nile.
- And on the sixth day, we celebrate Shavuot (see next page).

• **Gemini**, the sign of the twins, reminds us of two shepherds who turned into great leaders: Moses and David. Each had his own special abilities, and together they symbolize the Jewish people as a whole.

SPRING

SHAVUOT

Shavuot (Weeks) refers to the seven weeks of the Omer (see page 35) starting from the second day of Passover. Also known as Pentecost (fifty, in Greek, counting the number of days from the second day of Passover). The holiday is referred to with three additional names, describing the three reasons for the celebration:

1. Hag Hakatzir - celebrating the final wheat harvest.

2. Hag Habikkurim - ripening of first fruit to be taken to the Temple.

3. Hag Matan Torah - the time the law was given to the Israelites on Mount Sinai.

Shavuot is likened to a wedding, between the Jews and God. It is customary to eat dairy products and fruit, and on the first day of this two day holiday the Ten Commandments are recited. The Israelites were only able to listen to the first two commandments directly from God, since His presence was too awesome. The remaining commandments were told by Moses.

On the second day, the Book of Ruth is read. Ruth was the great-grandmother of King David, who was born and died on Shavuot. As part of the harvest festival, the Seven Kinds of produce of Israel are celebrated: Wheat, barley, grapes, figs, pomegranates, olives, and dates.

TAMMUZ

Days of rays of summer gold,
Lemonade and popsicles,
Far away from winter's cold
Riding on our bicycles.
Let's escape the scorching sun,
Hide beneath a shady tree.
Think of times that weren't so fun
When our people weren't so free.

Battle fought and battle lost
In this month we call Tammuz,
Burning city - holocaust!
No one could believe the news...
And today we cast our eyes
On a city made of gold.
In our hearts we hear the cries,
From those Summer days of old.

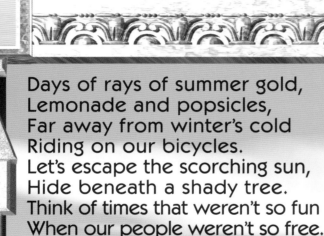

MOSES

CANCER

IN THE MONTH OF TAMMUZ

- It's name comes from the name of a popular Babylonian pagan god.

- On the sixteenth day, Aaron made the Golden Calf for the Israelites who thought Moses would never again return after forty days on Mount Sinai. They wanted a new god to lead them.

תמוז

SUMMER

41

- Bad things took place on the seventeenth day, so it was made a fast day: Moses broke the Tablets of the Law, and the Babylonians broke down the walls of Jerusalem, which led to the destruction of the Temple (see page 44).

- Cancer, the crab, is likened to Moses, who was drawn from water, and wandered for the rest of his life on the desert sand.

SUMMER

A V

Castles in the air,
City on a cloud,
Come up if you dare,
It's not so far out.
Pluck a piece of fluff,
Pick a blue of sky,
Mix up all this stuff,
Let me show you why.

Out of the sand
There will rise a wall.
Smooth it with your hand,
Help it grow real tall.
Watch a building grow
From your touch of love,
Watch the magic glow
On this day in Av.

42

IN THE MONTH OF AV

- It was decreed that the generation that left Egypt would not enter Israel.

- 40 years after leaving Egypt, Aaron, the first High Priest and Moses' brother, died on Mount Hor.

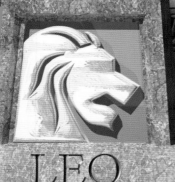

LEO

43

- On the ninth day, Tisha B'Av is observed (see next page).

- Leo, the lion, represents the Temple in Jerusalem which was known as Ariel - Lion of God. Also, the great kabbalist, Rabbi Isaac Luria who was known as HaAri (The Lion), died.

SUMMER

It was the ninth day in the month of Av, Tisha B'Av, when the spies that Moses sent into the land of Canaan returned, and claimed that the inhabitants were too powerful for the Israelites to conquer. When the people heard the report they began to cry and complain.

God declared: "You wept without a cause, I shall therefore make this day an eternal day of mourning for you."

And the Israelites were condemned to wander the desert for forty years.

44

Many terrible things took place on Tisha B'Av since, making this a sad day:

• The first Temple was destroyed by Nebuchadnezzar the Babylonian king in 586 B.C.E.

• The second Temple was destroyed by Titus and his Romans in the year 70.

• In the year 135 the fortress at Baytar was captured by the Romans, and Bar Kochvah and his followers were murdered (see page 35).

• In 1290 King Edward I of England banished the Jews. They were not readmitted until the 1600's.

• 150,000 Jews were exiled from Spain in 1492, in the beginning of the Spanish Inquisition, by King Ferdinand and Queen Isabella.

On the evening of Tisha B'Av, Lamentations from the book of Jeremiah are read. At the conclusion of the service the poems of Yehudah Ha'Levi are read, bringing hope to the exiled Jews.

Tu B'Av, the fifteenth day of Av, was celebrated as the grape harvest.

Young girls would wear white dresses and dance beneath the full moon, hoping to attract the young men watching. It was a happy day, especially so soon after the sad time of Tisha B'Av.

On Tu B'Av the forty years of wandering in the desert came to an end, marking a new beginning in the land of Israel.

AUGUST

E L U L

R G O

IN THE MONTH OF ELUL

- On the first day, Moses went up to Mount Sinai to receive the second tablets after he had smashed the first (see page 40).

- S'lihot, prayers for forgiveness, are said in preparation for the upcoming High Holidays (see page 8), and the shofar is sounded in the synagogue every weekday.

אלול

He saw that everything was night
And told the darkness, "go away!"
He made the morning bright with light,
He did this all in just One day.
The Second day He made the sky,
And on the Third the land and sea
And grass and plants which grew so high,
And lots of fruit on every tree.

The Fourth day brought the moon and sun,
The Fifth saw birds and swimming fish,
On day Six animals, one by one,
And then we came - it was His wish!
And God said everything was good,
And everything turned out so cool,
Yes, everything was like it should,
It started on this month - Elul!

47

- On the twenty-fifth day the creation of the world began.

- The name is an acronym for a verse from Song of Songs, "I am my beloved's and my beloved's mine", representing Israel's relationship with God.

- Virgo represents purity and innocence, as we strive to start with a clean slate for the coming year.

SUMMER